CIRCUS TRICKS
for **Your Dog**

CIRCUS TRICKS
for Your Dog

25 Crowd-Pleasers That Will
Make Your Dog a Star

Rick Martin

LARK BOOKS
A Division of
Sterling Publishing Co., Inc.
New York

Art Director:
Kristi Pfeffer

Editor:
Joanne O'Sullivan

Cover Design:
Kristi Pfeffer,
Orrin Lundgren

Photography:
Steve Mann
  (performance photography)
www.keithwright.com
  (cover photography)

Photo Styling:
Chris Bryant, Skip Wade

Illustrator:
Orrin Lundgren

Set Design:
Kristi Pfeffer,
Ben Betsalel

Associate Art Director:
Shannon Yokeley

Art Production Assistant:
Jeff Hamilton

Editorial Assistance:
Susan Kieffer,
Delores Gosnell

Editorial Intern:
David Squires

Library of Congress Cataloging-in-Publication Data

Martin, Rick, 1954-
  Circus tricks for your dog : 25 crowd-pleasers that will make your dog a star /
featuring Rick Martin and the tricky dogs. -- 1st ed.
      p. cm.
  Includes index.
  ISBN 1-57990-816-0 (pbk.)
  1. Dogs--Training. I. Title.
SF431.M445 2006
636.7'0835--dc22

                                                2006017010

10 9 8 7 6 5 4 3 2 1

First Edition

Published by Lark Books, A Division of
Sterling Publishing Co., Inc.
387 Park Avenue South, New York, N.Y. 10016

Text and illustrations © 2006, Lark Books
Photography © 2006, Lark Books, unless otherwise specified

Distributed in Canada by Sterling Publishing,
c/o Canadian Manda Group, 165 Dufferin Street
Toronto, Ontario, Canada M6K 3H6

Distributed in the United Kingdom by GMC Distribution Services,
Castle Place, 166 High Street, Lewes, East Sussex, England BN7 1XU

Distributed in Australia by Capricorn Link (Australia) Pty Ltd.,
P.O. Box 704, Windsor, NSW 2756 Australia

If you have questions or comments about this book, please contact:
Lark Books
67 Broadway
Asheville, NC 28801
(828) 253-0467

Manufactured in China

ISBN 13: 978-1-57990-816-4
ISBN 10: 1-57990-816-0

For information about custom editions, special sales, premium and corporate
purchases, please contact Sterling Special Sales Department at 800-805-5489
or specialsales@sterlingpub.com.

Contents

Introduction

Ladies and gentlemen, children of all ages, prepare yourselves to be amazed! Before your very eyes, you'll see your dog—faithful companion and precious pooch—transformed into a canine wonder, capable of such marvelous feats as speaking, dancing, jumping through hoops, and even riding a skateboard. How, you may ask, could such marvels be possible? Read on and the secrets of the circus dog will be revealed to you!

It seems that as long as dogs have kept company with humans, they've entertained them. More than 2,000 years ago, Plutarch wrote of a dog named Zoppico who performed tricks for Emperor Vespasian. Zoppico's best-known trick was to eat a piece of meat, then fall over and play dead, only to be brought back to life by imperial applause. You could say he was the first in a long line of clown dogs who've kept audiences amused ever since.

As a kid, I loved watching the circus-style animal acts on "The Ed Sullivan Show." Particularly memorable was an act featuring a black and white spaniel named Louie and his enthusiastic trainer. Louie was a droopy Spaniel who, in fact, did not actually do anything. As Louie sat there, slumped in funny positions, his trainer encouraged him to jump through a hoop. "You can do it, Louie!," he cheered, as Louie continued to slouch. That was the genius of the act—the role reversal between human and dog created great comedy, and motivated me to try dog training for myself, first for fun and later as a career.

Every dog has the potential to be an entertainer (and so does every human!). This book will show you how to work with your dog to bring out his or her hidden talents, and your own. If you're currently playing with your dog, observing her natural behavior, and praising her when she follows your instructions, you've already started trick training. From there, I'll show you how to teach your pup the basic commands that are the cornerstone of canine good behavior. Once your dog has a firm foundation in these essentials, you're both ready for the really fun stuff!

Dogs who execute difficult tricks with the ease, grace, precision, and cleverness of human beings!

The most astonishing feats by the best-trained dogs!

Your dog's breed and personality will play a role in determining which tricks are right for her. Is she energetic? Does he like to fetch? Does she follow her nose wherever she goes? Regardless of breed, every dog can learn certain types of tricks, and you may just be surprised at what your dog can do when given a challenge.

You may be satisfied doing your tricks at home just for the fun of it. But what if you and your little entertainer really want to put on a show? I'll offer you tips on developing your dog's "character," making a series of tricks into an act, and incorporating props and costumes into your routine. You'll find information on introducing your dog to an audience and using audience response to help improve your act. You'll even discover how to "go pro"—perform your act at local venues or even break into TV, movies, or advertising.

If you're patient, passionate, and persistent, your little showman might really become a star!

Whether you're under the big top or in your backyard, you can participate in the wonderful tradition of trick training; it's a fun way to bond with your dog. It will keep your dog sharp, keep you on your toes, and keep your friends amused. So what are you waiting for? Let the show begin!

Clever and remarkable acts to amaze and astound all beholders!

Getting Started

There are lots of reasons to train your dog—from basic house training to obedience to agility trials for competition. Dogs can be trained for helping professions such as guard dog, companion dog, or guide dog, or for jobs that take advantage of their natural abilities, such as tracking, hunting, or herding, and even bomb and drug detection. There's an old saying that claims, "There is no more contented creature than a dog with a job." It's really true. Dogs enjoy doing something useful and working in cooperation with humans. It's in their nature, and they are truly relaxed and satisfied when they've got an occupation.

Although there are many training books that will help you prepare your dog for agility trials and other competitive events, this book will focus on training your dog to entertain people (and if some other types of animals find your efforts amusing, that will be good, too). Training dogs to do tricks is fun and is free of the stress of house training or the pressure of competition. It's done primarily for the enjoyment of

human and dog, but it has some great side benefits as well, such as strengthening and exercise, both mentally and physically, for the dog, and increased bonding between human and dog. So why not give it a try? By simply observing and working with your dog's natural behavior, you'll be off to a great start.

A Star Is Born —Or Is She Bred?

Although your dog is certainly a star in your own estimation, you may wonder whether she has what it takes to perform tricks as an entertainer. Those in the know agree that most any dog (with the exception of those who are aggressive or quick to bite) can be successful in the glamorous world of show business. Young or old, big or small, smart or less-than-brilliant have already passed the audition just by being a dog.

Even timid pound puppies that were mistreated earlier in life can learn to be good performers (all of my performing dogs come from shelters). Training and performing can actually

be very therapeutic for a shy and fearful dog. The key is for you, the trainer, to help bring out your dog's star power.

You don't have to have amazing psychic abilities to "unleash" your dog's hidden potential. It all starts with the simple act of observation. If you pay attention, you just might find that your dog's natural behaviors can be molded into a performance piece.

For example, many dogs will stand up on their hind legs and do a little "feed me" dance when they see their human handling yummy foodstuffs. If this describes your dog, you may as well call it dancing and take credit for training him to do it! Some dogs will kick up the grass with their back paws after performing a toilet function. If you follow the correct training methods, you can get your dog to do it on command. (Note: It goes without saying that you must be careful to train for the back kicking and not the business that precedes it.) Whatever your dog's natural quirk or ability, you can use it as a starting point for trick training.

Pay attention, too, to your dog's natural energy level and personality. An energetic dog who loves to run, jump, and play catch will have an easier time learning a trick that requires agility, such as jumping through a hoop.

Beyond personality, breed plays a strong role in determining what your dog can and wants to do. The droopy basset hound, not known for its grace or jumping abilities, is expected to be slow, lazy, gentle, and maybe a little bit stubborn. Comedy is the basset's forte—this type of hound can really sink its teeth into a meaty clown role. When given a funny "script" to work with, a basset hound can be a standout performer.

The standard poodle, on the other hand, is known for its grace and high jumping ability, and it is expected to be quick, agile, smart, and cooperative.

Poodles, therefore, are most often trained for tricks requiring their natural agility skills. Note: That doesn't preclude them from going for the easy laugh by running under the hoop instead of jumping through it. It's funnier when the elegant poodle flubs the trick because the flub is unexpected.

Tiny toy dogs, such as Chihuahuas, can be surprisingly agile, and they're often trained for feats appropriate to their size, such as sitting up in the palm of the trainer's hand or balancing on their front paws with their rear ends up in the air—basically doggy handstands. Their short stature and unusual appearance also make them suitable for clowning, and they're often found dressed in bonnets, passing for "babies" being pushed in a carriage by another dog.

Sporting dogs such as retrievers, pointers, spaniels, and hounds have extra-super sniffing ability, and they can perform "mentalist" and magic tricks by picking out selected playing cards or numbered or lettered blocks. They can easily be trained to show off their amazing psychic prowess by picking up the last thing touched by a human hand or the one thing touched by a human other than the trainer.

So, as you can see, all dogs have something to offer in the way of entertainment.

Which Trick for Your Breed?

HOUND GROUP

Includes: Afghan Hound, American Foxhound, Basset Hound, Beagle, Bloodhound, Borzoi, Dachshund, English Foxhound, Greyhound, Irish Wolfhound, Rhodesian Ridgeback, Whippet, etc.

Best Tricks: *Anything that involves using their noses*

SPORTING GROUP

Includes: American Water Spaniel, Brittany, Cocker Spaniel, English Cocker Spaniel, English Setter, German Shorthaired Pointer, Golden Retriever, Irish Setter, Labrador Retriever, Pointer, Weimeraner

Best Tricks: *Energetic activities, such as jumping, retrieving*

WORKING GROUP

Includes: Akita, Alaskan Malamute, Black Russian Terrier, Boxer, Bullmastiff, Doberman Pinscher, Giant Schnauzer, Great Dane, Great Pyrenees, Komondor, Mastiff, Newfoundland, Rottweiler, Saint Bernard, Samoyed, Siberian Husky

Best Tricks: *Complex, multistep tasks*

TERRIER GROUP

Includes: Airedale Terrier, American Staffordshire Terrier, Border Terrier, Bull Terrier, Cairn Terrier, Irish Terrier, Kerry Blue Terrier, Miniature Schnauzer, Norfolk Terrier, Norwich Terrier, Parson Russell Terrier, Scottish Terrier, Skye Terrier, Welsh Terrier, Wire Fox Terrier

Best Tricks: *Acrobatics, comedy, tasks that require quick thinking*

TOY GROUP

Includes: Affenpinscher, Cavalier King Charles Spaniel, Chihuahua, Chinese Crested, English Toy Spaniel, Italian Greyhound, Japanese Chin, Maltese, Pekingese, Pomeranian, Poodle, Pug, Shih Tzu, Toy Fox Terrier, York Terrier
Best Tricks: Jumping, tasks that require agility, "speaking"

NON-SPORTING GROUP

Includes: American Eskimo Dog, Bichon Frise, Boston Terrier, Bulldog, Chinese Shar-Pei, Chow Chow, Dalmatian, French Bulldog, Keeshond, Lhasa Apso, Poodle
Best Tricks: Depends on breed

HERDING GROUP

Includes: Australian Shepherd, Belgian Shepherd, Border Collie, Bouvier des Flandres, Cardigan Welsh Corgi, Collie, German Shepherd, Old English Sheepdog, Pembroke Welsh Corgi, Shetland Sheepdog
Best Tricks: Good at following most instructions

Timing Is Everything In Show Biz

Even the youngest of puppies can, and should, start trick "school" right away. Most puppies are thrilled by human attention and will run to anyone who seems friendly. You might as well start calling the pup by name and praising her when she comes to you—that's essentially all the training you need to do for the "Come" command.

If you are starting with a grown dog, or an adopted dog from an animal shelter, you will want to make sure the dog is relaxed and comfortable with you before you start training for obedience and tricks. A nervous or fearful dog most likely got that way from bad experiences with abusive people and may need weeks or even months before being ready to learn tricks. If your doggy is happy and confident, then there is no reason to delay the start of trick training.

It's important to keep the training sessions fun for the dog. It's much better to do three 10-minute sessions, a few hours apart, than one 30-minute session all at once. Slow, steady progress is what you are after, and you want to avoid letting things get stressful for you or the dog. However, it is important for you to be the boss and set the agenda. Dogs feel most comfortable when the chain of command is clearly understood by all involved.

Like many people, dogs are most relaxed and cooperative when they feel like they are working with good managers. Dogs are also most comfortable with a predictable routine.

They like to eat and go for walks at the same time each day, and they will enjoy a steady training schedule as well.

It's not necessary to do your training sessions at the exact same time each day, but if you keep to a basic schedule, your dog will be raring to go when it's training time. Some dogs might benefit from a day off now and then, which may make them more appreciative of the training time spent with you. But there are no hard rules about how many days a week to work with a dog. Each dog is different, and will let you know whether you are working him too much by being uninterested in an activity he previously enjoyed.

Timing is everything in show biz, and the time to train performing dogs is before, during, and after the performance. Training while "on stage" and

in front of an audience is especially helpful, because it helps both you and the doggy performers work out the timing necessary to get the best reaction from the audience, who will likely be family and friends (they will be patient and understanding as you get your act together). When they do laugh and clap, you can try the click-and-treat technique (see page 17) to reinforce the desired behavior.

You may be wondering how long it will take to teach your dog to do circus tricks. The answer is, it all depends. Different dogs learn at different rates, different tricks take different lengths of time to learn, and different trainers train different dogs at different rates. Jumping through a hoop is a fairly easy trick for most dogs to learn, and some may even learn to do it in two or three sessions. But some dogs will take weeks to learn the hoop trick.

For some dogs, you'll need to break down each trick into its smallest component and teach the trick one step at a time. Slowly build the trick a step at a time for as long as it takes, which will be exactly as long as it takes.

Training Basics

Although dog training philosophy and methodology has changed a lot over the years, dog trainers today mostly agree on a few basics.

Dog training usually has two purposes: You want to teach the dog to do good things, and you want to train her *not* to do bad things. Bad things include running away from you and refusing to come when called, barking at inappropriate times, biting (which can be playful or mean-spirited), and destroying things, such as shoes and slippers.

Whether your purpose is the former or the latter, it's widely accepted that dogs respond best to positive reinforcement. Negative reinforcement will bring negative results. Hitting or kicking a dog will not get him to behave or perform—it will just intimidate him and make him flinch and cower. Bad behavior on the part of the trainer is not likely to correct bad behavior on the part of the dog; hitting isn't teaching. Once a dog becomes nervous and fearful of the person working with him, the game is pretty much over. Dogs carry this fear and anxiety with

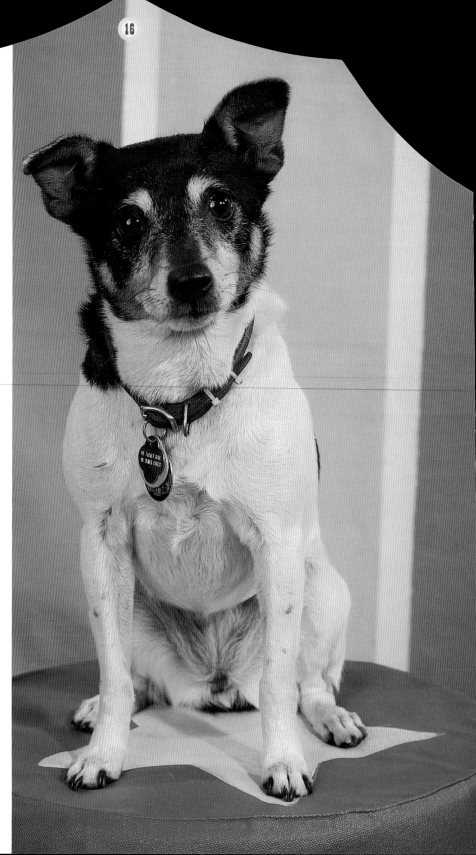

them for the rest of their lives. Dogs that have been abused can recover to some degree over time, but they will almost always continue to tell the story of an unhappy past with their body language, such as carrying their tails between their legs and walking with a crouched, slinky posture when they are around people they don't feel comfortable with. Positive reinforcement, on the other hand, contributes to creating a happy, well-adjusted dog and a good relationship between dog and trainer.

What exactly does positive reinforcement mean? It means rewarding your dog with something he likes—praise and petting, a treat, a favorite toy—when he displays the behavior that you're asking for. The reward lets the dog know that he's done well and that you're pleased. He'll be eager to repeat the behavior to please you again. This is the cornerstone of training—getting your dog to repeat a desirable behavior.

Clicker Training

It's certainly possible to train your dog using your voice and a combination of positive training techniques, but you do have another option: clicker training.

In my opinion, the clicker is the greatest dog-training tool since sliced baloney. The basic idea behind it is simple. The clicker, a small plastic object about the size of a matchbox, has a bendable metal part that makes a cricket-click sound. When you press the piece with a finger, you make the sound, which is used to help the dog identify the behavior that you want from her.

Although you may eventually be able to get the same results without it, the clicker provides a reliable measure of consistency, which in turn gives you a better chance of consistent results from your dog. Also, once your dog has the hang of the trick, you can retire the clicker, and she will be able to proceed with the trick without it.

Here's an example of how you can effectively use the clicker for training.

Let's say you are trying to teach your dog to jump up onto a box. You'd follow these four steps:

1 Give a Command
Specifically, for this trick, your command could be "Jump up," delivered (by the trainer) in an enthusiastic and encouraging manner. Dogs are very sensitive to human speech patterns, and it is not helpful to shout a command in a harsh or threatening way.

2 Click Your Clicker
Have the clicker ready to click as soon as your dog does anything that moves him closer to jumping on the box. This might be putting a paw on the box or even moving just a little closer to it. Rather than waiting for your dog to guess correctly what you are jabbering about with your "Jump up" command, give him some hints. You could pat the surface of the stand to show him where you want him to go. Some dogs seem to understand that hint, but holding a food treat out in front of his nose to lead him up to and onto the box will almost always work.

3 Give a Treat
Hold the treat out as a lure. When the dog puts a paw or two onto the box to get close enough to the treat to take it, click, and let him have the treat.

4 Give Praise
Say "Good dog" and give some affection.

The key is to click just as the dog does what you want and then quickly follow up with the treat and the praise. The sound of the click helps the dog pinpoint exactly what it is you want him to do, and what will get him the treat and praise. Some trainers will use a favorite toy as a reward instead of food. If that works for you and your dog, that's fine. However, some dogs are so crazy about their toys that the toy may be a distraction, making it difficult for the dog to think about anything else.

The Basic Commands: Sit, Stay, and Come

Before you can effectively teach a dog to do tricks, you'll need to have the basic behavior commands under control: "Sit," "Stay," and "Come" must be mastered before your dog can do something like dance or even wave a paw. Here's how to get started.

Sit

The sit command essentially means, "Stop running around acting like a wild animal, and no, we are not going to play tug of war right now." Note: If a dog is doing a good sit, he can't be doing any of those other things. He can be thinking about them, and that can be a problem, so you're going to have to include a "Sit" and a "Pay Attention to Me" component.

Teaching a dog to sit will be a good training experience for both of you, and the technique you use here will likely be carried through the entire training process. You will be using treats (such as little pieces of food), praise (such as "good doggy"), and, if you so choose, a clicker.

Setting the Stage

To teach a dog to sit, you might want to have the dog on the leash and standing by your side. (You won't need the leash much for training after you get the basics down.) There are several schools of thought on what to do next: push down the rump, lift the chin, or dangle a treat in front of the nose. I advocate doing a little of each.

1 Gently push down on the dog's rump while holding a hand under his chin (see figure 1).

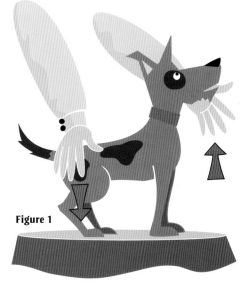

Figure 1

2 Give the command "Sit," and gently push down on the dog's rump. As his rump moves toward the sitting position, you can click, and then give praise or a food treat, or both. "Sit" is such an easy trick that you may just end up waiting until the dog is sitting before clicking and rewarding.

Perfecting the Act

1 Although sitting is easy, *staying* seated may be a real challenge for high-energy dogs. You'll want to train the dog to hold the sitting position until given a command *not* to sit. As long as the dog is sitting nicely, you can continue with the praise, saying things such as "Good doggy, look how nice you're sitting." If the dog starts to lift his rump up off the floor, you will need to let him know that he's committing a no-no. Saying "no, no" in a loud and

firm (but not threatening) voice will be your primary tool of correction. The key is to be firm, but not mean, and authoritative, but not intimidating. This is really the essence of dog training, and this is why people have trouble training their dogs. The dog has to take your commands and corrections seriously. If he thinks you don't mean business with your commands, then he will not obey unless he wants to.

Of course, you do not want to hit the dog or handle her with any sort of violence, but your corrections must be delivered with some force and authority.

2 This "no, no" correction will be an all-purpose signal to your dog to stop doing whatever is causing you, the trainer, to say no.

As soon as the dog sits back down, it's "good doggy" time again. To recap: Give praise for the good behavior and say "no, no" for the not-so-good behavior.

Note: Some clever pooches will try to turn the tables on the trainer by deliberately lifting their rump from a good sit just to get the praise that will come when they get back into position. For this reason, it's best not to use a food treat when cor-

recting a no-no. The food treat will help motivate the sly dog to mess up deliberately in hopes of getting extra yummies for being good again. Another doggy scam is to act dumb and pretend not to understand the command. Neither of these canine rackets is difficult for the trainer to get around. Just keep at the training techniques and pretty much every dog will come around and start to cooperate. The key is making it fun for you and your dog and keeping at it.

Stay

Teaching a dog to stay is really just teaching him to stay in the sit position. He is "staying" as long as he is sitting. If you have the sit command down, it's time to work on "Stay."

Setting the Stage

1 Get your dog into the sit position, praise him, face him, hold your palm toward him, and

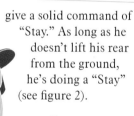

Figure 2

give a solid command of "Stay." As long as he doesn't lift his rear from the ground, he's doing a "Stay" (see figure 2).

2 Back away a little at a time while repeating the "Stay" command. If your dog starts to get up, quickly say "no, no," using an appropriate tone of voice—not harsh and threatening, but authoritative and commanding. If your dog is supposed to be sitting and staying and he gets up and walks to you, go toward him while saying "no" in a somewhat severe tone. You can take him by the collar and put him back in his original

sit spot and command him to "Sit." When he sits, it's "good doggy" once again. If you click, treat, and praise on a correction like this, the dog may learn that breaking the sit and stay will get a reward. You'll have to use your judgment and adapt your training techniques to your dog. Once the dog is sitting again, give the "Stay" command, the hand signal, and slowly back away. Watch closely, and if your dog starts to lift his rear off the floor even a little bit, immediately bark a "no" or two.

Perfecting the Act

Continue practicing this command with consistency, and your dog should master it fairly quickly.

Come

Teaching a dog to come to you is very easy, unless the dog doesn't *want* to come to you.

Setting the Stage

1 After you are satisfied with the sitting and staying, you can call your dog to you in a happy, friendly way. If she bounds over to you, then make a big fuss with lots of praise. You probably won't need a treat for this and clicking is up to you. If your dog doesn't come to you or wanders around, then you can try attaching a long leash or light rope to her collar.

2 Get your dog to sit and stay and then give the "Come" command. If your dog doesn't come to you, you can gently pull on the leash and guide the dog to do the right thing (see figure 3). When she gets to you, it's "good doggy" time.

Note: Some dogs will run wild when off the leash and ignore their trainer's commands to come. Some dogs will try to make a game of

"catch me if you can" and may even run right up to the trainer and scoot away just as the trainer tries for a grab. This is great fun for most dogs, but it is not a good game, and it's not safe. An out-of-control dog running wild could get lost or hit by a car. It's very important for safety and for general training that your dog respects your authority as leader of the pack.

Perfecting the Act

1 Until your dog is dependably coming to you immediately when called, you might want to use a piece of thin, light twine tied to a clip and attached to her collar. Hardware stores sell a type of twine, which is thin, light nylon

Figure 3

and a bright color. This twine works great for training because it's so light in weight that the dog will barely notice it. Start with a piece as long as 50 feet, if necessary. Make sure it's firmly attached to a typical dog leash clip, and clip it to the dog's collar.

2 If your dog is running around out of control or running away from you, you can shout "no" and stomp on the twine. This will stop the dog in his tracks and allow you to catch up to him. Tie a few knots in your end of the twine so that it can't slide under your shoe as you step on it. This twine shows the dog that you are in control whether you are within arm's reach or not.

Over time, you can cut the twine shorter and shorter until it's just a 1-foot-long (30.5 cm) piece dangling from the dog's collar. Of course, this little 1-foot (30.5 cm) piece won't enable you to get control of your dog, but the dog probably won't figure that out. Some rambunctious dogs have to wear the piece of twine for weeks until they can behave without it.

Putting on the Dog: Working with Costumes and Props

There are plenty of great tricks your dog can perform without using any props, such as dancing, waving, bowing, balancing, crawling…well, that's about it. If you choose to expand your repertoire, though, you'll probably want to incorporate some of these extras into your act.

Costumes

People are of two minds about dogs and costumes. Some find it irresistibly cute to dress a dog in antlers or a holiday sweater, but they draw the line at putting their dog in a clown hat and ruff. Some, especially those involved in canine freestyle (see page 106), will happily dress up in a costume to match their dog's so that both can participate in the fun. Others feel outfitting a dog in any way is demeaning to him, regardless of the purpose.

The bottom line should always be whether the dog is comfortable or whether he resists the costume. Can it cause him to trip or get snagged during the performance? In other words, is it a safe and appropriate outfit for your dog? Sometimes a dog will show initial distrust or confusion with a costume, but then settle down after getting used to it. Other dogs will not wear anything, under any circumstances. You'll really have to test it out on your dog to find out.

Any costume that restricts a dog's air passages, vision, or ability to relieve himself is not acceptable no matter how cute or funny you think it looks. Always keep safety and comfort in mind first.

If your dog does seem amenable to being dressed up, a costume can be a fun and an easy way to make your show look professional. In general, in terms of dog costumes, less is more. A scarf (bandana), hat, or some type of vest that allows all limbs to move freely is appropriate. You can purchase costumes made specifically for dogs at costume stores or pet supply stores (there are many online sources), make your own, or adjust a child's

hat or costume for your dog. If your dog shows a little initial resistance, you might try offering a treat when she wears it for longer than a second, building that positive association with the costume.

Your dog's costume should reflect his "character" (That is, is your dog a clown? An acrobat? A daredevil?). Should you decide to perform your act for an audience, you, the trainer, should wear a costume, too. Your costume should reflect your character—are you the "clown" that the dog takes advantage of? Are you the celebrated ringmaster working with dazzling creatures? Your appearance will also have a big impact on the overall effect of the performance.

Props

CARPET

When it comes to props, a piece of carpet is a good place to start. You might want to consider purchasing an inexpensive area rug measuring 6 x 9 feet (183 x 274 cm) or a piece of carpet runner measuring 2 x 10 feet (61 x 305 cm).

The carpet gives your dog traction to jump and acts as a bit of a crash pad for landing the jumps. A carpet also gives your performance a stage, and this helps convince an audience that you and your dog know what you are doing. The carpet will help the dog identify the area within which he is expected to stay while performing.

The long, narrow carpet runner will allow the dog to take a greater running start for tricks such as jumping through a hoop or over a barrier.

Any shape carpet can be used as a comedy prop, and it's very easy to teach a dog to unroll a rug (see page 84).

HOOP

Jumping through a hoop is a good trick to try early in training. You can purchase a lightweight plastic hula hoop in several different sizes. These are perfectly safe for your dog—the lightweight, somewhat flexible plastic won't harm her if she bangs a paw into the hoop while jumping through.

If you want a fancier hoop, you can get a fisherman's saltwater landing net, also available in several sizes. These lightweight hoops made of shiny aluminum will need to be altered a bit for your purposes: cut off and discard the string net, leaving the hoop and handle. You may need to use a hacksaw to make the handle a little shorter.

You can also make a holder for your hoop by drilling the appropriate size hole into a block of wood and sticking the end of the handle into the hole,

with the wood block acting as a weighted base. You will have to experiment to get the right size block of wood, and you should try to make this prop somewhat balanced, so it will fall over easily if the dog hits it while jumping through.

For further protection for your dog, you can easily pad the rim of the hoop with foam pipe insulation available at hardware stores. This material is already split lengthwise, so it's easy enough to cut it to the proper length and fit it around your hoop. It will stay in place without glue—just arrange it so the split is on the outer part of the hoop.

For extra flare, you can attach comedy cardboard fire (you can make this yourself with a corrugated plastic craft material found in arts and craft stores) by just pushing it into the split in the foam.

HURDLES

If you want your dog to jump over hurdles, you can make nice little fences out of 1-inch (2.5 cm)-diameter PVC plumbing pipe. You probably won't even need to glue the parts, because they usually fit together snuggly. Once you are set on a design, it's easy enough to make the prop permanent using PVC cement.

STAND

Circus lions and tigers almost always remain on some sort of stand in between performing tricks. This type of "seat" works well for performing doggies as well (see above). An audience will be duly impressed just by the fact that your dog stays on her stand until called, and it's a great way to solidify the "Sit" and "Stay" commands.

If you are working with a small dog under 25 pounds, (11.3 kg), a plastic or resin outdoor end table from the garden department of a hardware store is ideal. A bigger dog needs a bigger table or box, and you'll have to be creative to find something that is big enough for the dog to lie down on, light enough for you to move around, and hopefully attractive enough to add to the look of your stage set-

ting. It's easy enough to disguise an everyday object with fabric or other materials you might find in a craft store.

BARREL

A rolling barrel can be made with two bicycle wheels of equal size. You'll use the rims only— no spokes or hubs or tires.

Attach the ends of wood lathe strips to the inside rim of the bike wheels using small nuts and bolts, going through the spoke holes of the wheels. Cut the pieces of lathe to exactly the length that you want for your barrel's width.

Make sure you cut all of the pieces of wood exactly the same length, and drill screw holes in both ends at exactly the same distance from the edge of the wood.

Hold the bike wheel hoops up on their edge, like they would be on the back end of a tricycle, and lay a strip of wood lathe between them. Screw the strip into place at the six o'clock position, and then do the same thing at the twelve o'clock position.

Once the whole drum is completed, you can cover the outside surface with low-pile carpet to give the dog a good traction surface. If you want something fancier, cover the drum in either the same color carpet as your stage surface carpet or use a complementary color. It's your show, so make it look however you and the dog want it to look.

The Big Picture: Creating an Act and Developing Your Dog's "Character"

Once you've got a few tricks down, think about developing a series of tricks into an act and figuring out where you, as the trainer, fit into the act.

The art of performance is a big subject, and is much too large to be covered in the scope of this book. It is better learned by observing and learning from a variety of artists performing in different fields. Watch street performers, magicians, jugglers, musicians, and mimes, and learn how they develop their acts and work a crowd. (You can learn a lot about performance from TV and movies, but you won't learn how to handle a live audience there.) Go to every circus that comes to town—everything you need to know is at the circus. Here are a few tried-and-true principles that you'll find useful as you develop your dog act.

Any variety act should tell some sort of simple story, and the story should have a beginning, a middle, and an end. A good basic story for a dog act is: "Look at this! My dog can do some tricks. Isn't this fun?" Another story could be: "Look at this! I tried to train my dog to do some tricks, but he's stubborn and naughty. Isn't this funny?" These stories are not so much told by what the performer says, as by what happens and develops during the act. It's important for the audience to figure out the story for themselves, and it's your job to give them the clues they need.

An effective entertainer (including a dog entertainer) should have an easily recognized character and should behave in ways that seem to fit that character. Many successful circus dog acts feature big, graceful dogs running and jumping and performing all sorts of impressive acrobatic tricks. Some of these traditional dog acts include one or two little dogs that serve as comic relief, getting solid laughs by running under a barrier after all of the big dogs have jumped over it. Presented properly, this simple bit of silliness will get the laugh every time: the little dog obviously can't jump as high as the big dogs, and when the little dog solves the problem by running under the hurdle, the audience gets a glimpse of the dog's personality, and a character

starts to develop. The strongest laughs a comedy dog can get from an audience come from pretending to be naughty and out of control. The "bad doggy character," who is uncooperative and makes a monkey of his trainer, is comedy gold, though complicated to achieve. As you continue to define the performing dog's character, you'll get stronger audience reactions (smiles, chuckles, guffaws, and belly laughs), setting things up for the ultimate in laughter, "The Boffo Laff."

When performing with your dog in front of an audience, you will actually be playing the part of a dog trainer during the act. You'll need to establish a stage character for yourself early on in the performance. Circus lion tamers traditionally play the part of the brave master, commanding the wild beasts to perform. You could do that, or you could make it a comedy act and play the part of a clown. Your stage character can speak to the audience or silently communicate with them through mime. These stereotypical circus types are useful as a starting point for developing your onstage persona.

You'll want to save your best trick for the end of your show. Even if it's just jumping through a hoop, it can be presented as an effective grand finale stunt if you build up to it and "sell" it to the crowd. You do this by making a big deal out of getting the hoop lined up and ready, getting the dog lined up and ready, and possibly having the audience or onstage volunteers count down and/or give a comedy drum roll, using their hands to drum on themselves.

Don't be afraid to take a bow and ask for applause by holding your arms out with your palms pointed up. Make the dog the star of the show and ask the audience to clap for her. Teach your dog to take a bow and you'll have the crowd right where you want them. And if you want to pass the hat for donations, now is the time.

Tricky Business: Going Pro

More than likely you started trick training with no greater aspiration than to amuse yourself, your friends, and your dog. But during the course of training, you might find that not only does your dog excel at certain tricks but he also truly seems to thrive on entertaining, and that you're having a blast, too. The thought might enter your mind: Could we have a future with this?

It's certainly possible, and plenty of people have earned money with dog acts, but the key to commercial success has much more to do with understanding show business than knowing how to train dogs. Your dog is capable of performing some impressive tricks, but is it a show? Can you hold an audience's attention for 20 minutes or longer? Will anybody be willing to pay you for your performance?

There is only one way to find out, and that's to try it and see what happens, learning from your experiences and adapting your routine until you get it together. Here are some tips to get you started.

Introducing A Crowd

Chances are, you've done your training at home—just the two of you, perfecting your act. So how will your performing pooch react when she has an audience? If you want your dog to be able to perform for a crowd, it's best to do as much of the training in front of people as possible.

Family and friends are fine, but strangers are even better for getting you and your dog used to doing your thing in public. Public parks are a great place to get used to working around distractions, and you very well could draw a little crowd of interested onlookers. You might even try other public areas, such as a boardwalk or a sidewalk in front of a shopping area, but first see whether a permit is necessary or you may find yourself trying to persuade the police (or nearby shop owners) that your show is not a public nuisance. You may try entering events or

contests sponsored by local dog clubs or other organizations; the more experience you can get, the better.

For your first few times, you might be nervous, and a big crowd could make things worse. A small audience of kids and their parents could be all you need. As you get more confident, try to get people who seem interested to come fairly close to you and commit themselves to watching your show. Some people will want to watch from a distance, and that's not so helpful to you because you won't be able to learn anything from those standing far away. And that brings us to a very important point: Pay careful attention to audience members and see how they react to what you and the dog are doing. What makes

them laugh and clap, and what makes them stand there with their arms folded across their chests with a sourpuss mug on their faces? What makes them turn and walk away? This will give you great feedback for improving future performances.

Taking Your Show on the Road

Assuming your act is a success, you'll probably want to consider opening it up to a wider audience or, as they say in show business, taking your show on the road.

"Selling" a dog trick act is not unlike any other sort of business you might start. You'll need the basics: a business card and, if you're really serious about it, professionally created signage and marketing materials, such as high-quality photos of your act, brochures or postcards, or a website. If you want to move beyond the impromptu performance at the park, there are several options to try for your first bookings: local rec centers or community centers, kids' groups (such as scout troops), elementary schools, senior citizen homes, churches and temples, camps, etc. When you're starting out, you may want to offer your show free of charge. This gives you an opportunity to learn and polish your act. If you want to become even a part-time professional dog act, perform in front of a live crowd as often as possible.

To create a professional impression, have all of your props on some sort of wagon or cart. Decorate the cart to look like a fairytale coach or circus train car and wear a complementary costume so that you can make a big entrance—it gets the crowd excited before you and your dog or dogs have even done a trick. If you have big dogs, they might be able to help pull the cart; if you have little dogs, they might be able to ride on the cart. Outline your "stage" area with a stout piece of rope—a colored rope is better than a plain one, and hardware stores sell all kinds of nice, thick colorful rope by the foot (you might

need a piece about 30 feet [9 m] long, but only you know what your stage should look like).

If you use music in your show (and why wouldn't you?), have a battery-powered boom box on hand because it's not likely you will be able to plug anything into a wall outlet. Choose peppy music that will get your crowd going and keep them energized, but make sure it's not so loud that it overshadows your performance or makes it difficult for the audience to focus on the act. Make sure you use the same music while practicing with the dogs to provide continuity for them.

The Big Time: Advertising, TV, and Movies

Lassie, Beethoven, that Taco Bell dog...do you dream of seeing your dog on the big or small screen like these celebrity pooches? A well-trained dog that can perform tricks and is comfortable around a variety of people and in a variety of situations certainly has a shot

at becoming an animal model or performer.

The easiest way to explore these high-profile opportunities is to hire an agent who specializes in animal talent. The agent will help develop your dog's "resume" (which outlines her physical characteristics, past experience, and talent), help you get "head shots" to send out with it, find auditions for you, and negotiate contracts for you. Animal talent agents can be found either through dog clubs or organizations or by doing an Internet search. But beware—you should always check the agent's references first. Anyone who asks you for money up front is more than likely trying to take you and your dog for a ride rather than on an audition. If you feel more comfortable handling your dog's career on your own, you'll probably still need some help making contacts in the industry. Again, you might turn to dog clubs or organizations to get a list of contacts started.

ON WITH

Now that you have the knowledge, it's time to start working on the skills. In the following section of the book, you'll find 23 tricks to teach your little star, from feats of agility to classic clown capers. Whether your plan is to do tricks in your living room or take your act all the way to the big time, this is the place to start. Your little dog is waiting in the wings, just looking for a chance to shine.

THE SHOW

He's the flashy frontman who gets the crowd going. He's got the looks, the moves, and the attitude to capture everyone's attention. With a little encouragement, your dog can be an MC, performing little tricks that get big applause. Teach him to sit up for an audience, speak out loud, "wave" his paw, and take a bow. Once he's comfortable with his place in the spotlight, you'll have no trouble teaching him other, even more spectacular tricks.

CEREMONIES

Speak or Sing

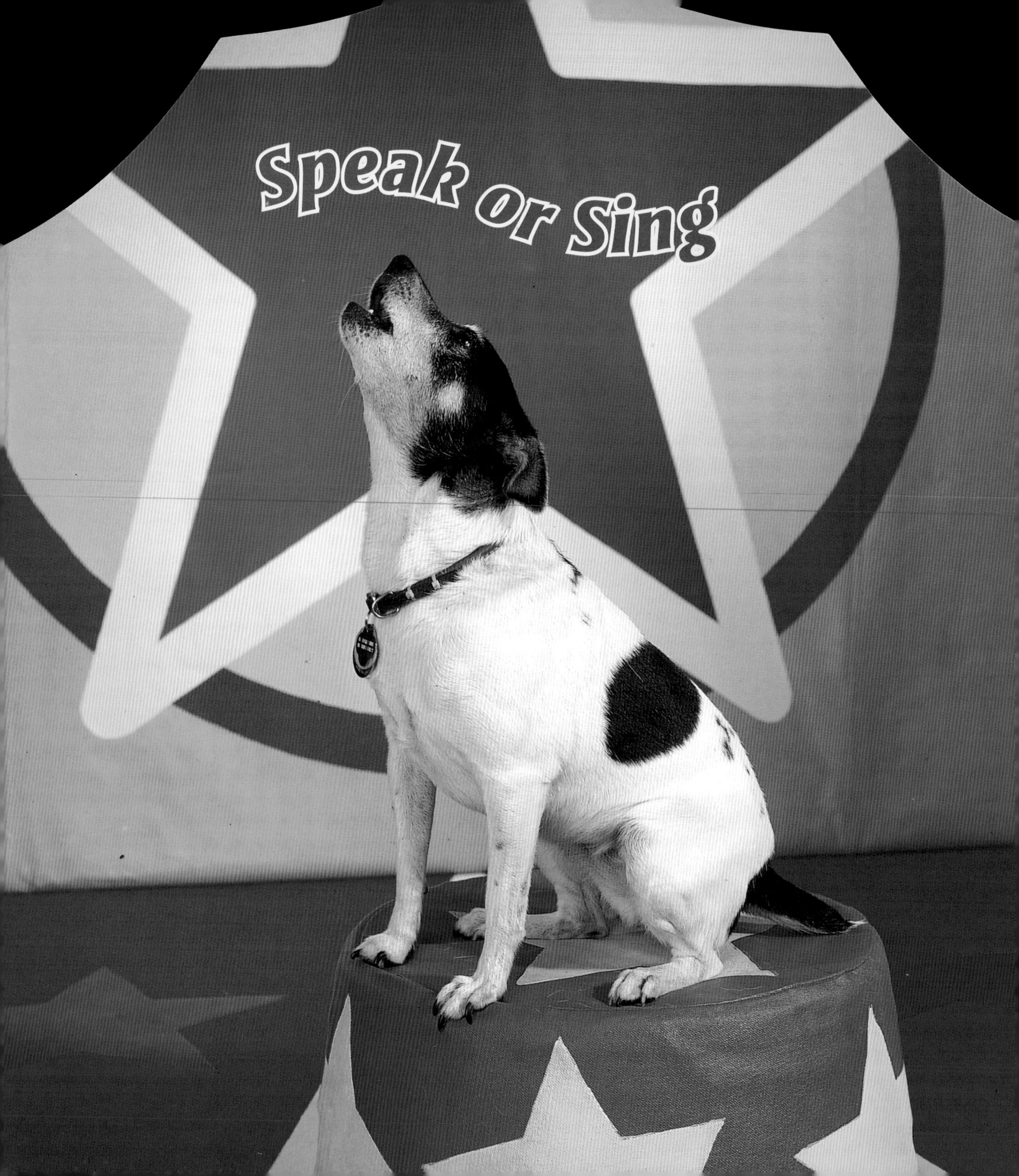

An MC's voice is what really gets the audience's attention.
You can train your little star to steal the spotlight by barking on cue.
This trick requires eye contact, voice commands, and hand signals.

Setting the Stage

1 Find something your dog likes, such as a toy or small treats. Secure her with a leash and hold the toy or treats out of range. You'll need to excite your dog so that she barks. As soon as she makes a sound, reward and praise her.

2 Continue encouraging your dog to bark using the "Speak" command. Reward and praise her after each bark, and say "Good speak" while petting her. Gradually, you can try taking the dog off the leash as you practice the trick.

Perfecting the Act

Begin to add a hand signal, such as a snap near your mouth or a raised index finger, and continue the encouraging procedure until the dog responds quickly to the command (see figure 4). Break eye contact when you want the dog to stop barking.

Best For: Any

Tip: It can help to encourage your dog to speak for positive things, such as for a meal or a walk or even to be let outside. If your dog barks out of turn, ignore her by turning your back to her or withholding affection until she stops. You may also find it useful to teach the dog a "Shhh" command. After asking your dog to speak, simply avert your eyes and stomp your foot. Reward your dog when she stops barking. Add a hand and voice command appropriately.

Figure 4

Train your dog to sit up and get noticed.
Although it may appear to be a simple trick, it's a bit complicated
—your dog will need to build up his back and leg muscles to
hold this position successfully. Frequent repetition is the key to helping him
learn to balance his weight on his hips and tail.

Setting the Stage

1 Have your dog sit in front of you. Use your hand or a treat as the target. Place your hand slightly above your dog's head so that he has to lift his front paws off the ground in order to touch your hand (see figure 5). As your dog lifts his head, say "Sit up! Good!" Offer a treat or reward only when his front legs come off the ground.

2 Slowly raise your hand higher until your dog is completely on his back legs. Don't raise your hand too high, or the dog will have to stand up to touch it. His back legs should not be extended.

Figure 5

Perfecting the Act

1 As you continue to train your dog for this trick, and his back and leg muscles strengthen, add a "Stay" or "Hold it" command. Never have him stay in position for longer than a minute.

Tip: If your dog has trouble balancing, you can try two things to help: You can place him in a corner so he can use the walls for balance or you can stand behind him to help him.

2 Your dog may also try to extend his front paws. If so, gently pull his front paws toward his chest and reward him for keeping them there.

Best For: Sporting, Non-Sporting, Mixed, Herding, Terrier, Working, Hound

Sit up on Hind Legs

You can probably teach your dog to shake hands in just one or two three-minute sessions—that's how easy it is to do. You'll start off using treats, but eventually your dog will do it without any incentive other than your praise.

Setting the Stage

1 First, get your dog into the sitting position (see page 18). Once he's sitting, reach down and lift his paw, then say "Shake." When he extends his paw into your hand, reward him with a treat and praise him, saying something like, "Good shake, good shake." Release his paw and repeat.

2 The next step will be to get him to give you his paw without your actually reaching for it—in other words, let him come to you. If he doesn't, you'll have to repeat grabbing the paw and lifting it yourself.

3 Keep rewarding him with a treat when he does extend his paw on the "Shake" command. Eventually you will be able to forgo the treat.

Best For: Any

Wave Your Paw

A true performer will always engage the crowd with a welcoming wave. This trick is a follow-up to the Shake Hands trick (see page 40).

Setting the Stage

1 Make sure that your dog is comfortable with the "Shake" command first. Once he has that down, have him sit next to you, and face him. Give him a cue that you want him to shake hands, or tell him verbally.

2 When he lifts his paw to shake, instead of meeting his paw, lift your hand higher so that he has to reach up, but don't let him reach your hand. Say "Wave" and reward him (see figure 6). You may also want to demonstrate for your dog what waving is, or move your hand back and forth above his paw so that he will try to follow the motion.

3 Continue this process again, saying "Wave" every time you lift your hand up higher and he tries to meet it. He will start to produce a waving motion. Reward him each time.

Wave!

Figure 6

Perfecting the Act

This trick is a great "starter" for your act. You might use the commands "Wave Hello" or "Wave Goodbye" so that your dog will respond with greetings on command.

Best For: Any

Every great performer must know how to take a bow.
This trick is a natural extension of the position dogs take when
they invite you to play—they bow by lowering their front end to the ground while
keeping their hips elevated. If you happen to catch your dog in the act, you may
easily train him by commanding "Bow," and praising him enthusiastically.
However, the trick can also be taught following these instructions.

Setting the Stage

1 First, get your dog to stand in front of you. Place one hand under the dog's tuck-up (the underside section between the chest and the hindquarters) and one hand a few inches under his chin (see figure 7).

2 Encourage your dog to touch your hand (the one that's under his chin) with his nose. Reward him with a treat and praise him when he does.

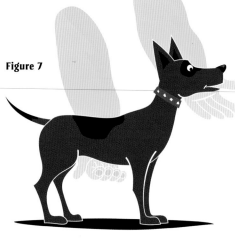

Figure 7

3 Continue training by lowering the hand underneath your dog's chin by several inches at a time, and rewarding your dog each time he makes a downward motion toward the hand. Praise him each time until the dog goes all the way to the ground.

4 Slowly remove the target hand just before it gets to the ground. Continue until your dog will bow with just a hand motion, then add the verbal command "Bow."

5 Remove your hand from the tuck-up and encourage your dog to repeat the motion without lying down.

Perfecting the Act

1 Increase the difficulty by increasing the duration of the trick. You may add a "Hold it" or "Stay" command, as well as a release command, such as "Okay" or "Up." If you prefer, applause and praise may also serve as a release.

2 Praise your dog each time he improves a step. If he doesn't improve, don't praise as much. Simply say, "Let's try harder." If your dog won't stay in the bow position, don't reprimand him. Just stop praising him and gently reposition him into the bow position. Resume praise. Continue practicing the trick until he doesn't need help to get into the bow position.

Best For: Any

Take a Bow

Dog Stars

The Dog and Pony Show

Nowadays, "dog and pony show" has come to mean any sort of small-scale but showy performance, from a business presentation to a politician's speech. But circus insiders know that the term is based on a classic circus act that brings two talented species together to entertain and amuse crowds.

In the 1890s (often thought of as the heyday of the American circus), there were dozens of small, traveling "wagon" circuses competing with the big-league outfits, such as Barnum & Bailey Circus and Ringling Brothers Circus. They often didn't have the staff, equipment, or budget to put on major shows, so they settled for smaller spectacles, such as animal acts. Among their standard offerings was the dog and pony show.

What tricks did the acts consist of? Single or multiple dogs "rode" the ponies as jockeys, and the ponies and dogs raced each other or climbed stairs. The ponies danced, skipped rope, did high-dives off of platforms, or leapt over each other. The dogs danced, "sang," counted, and leapt through flames. The show also featured an animal role reversal, with the dogs doing something traditionally associated with ponies and vice versa; often the dogs pulled carts, and the horses jumped through flaming hoops. Occasionally, the dog and pony show was a sort of sideshow freak act, featuring a tiny miniature pony and a giant dog that towered over it.

Left: An anonymous dog and pony act from the past.

Dog and pony stars pose for a publicity shot.

Dog and pony shows grew in popularity around the turn of the 20th century. Perhaps the best-known outfit was the Gentry Brothers Circus. The troupe started as a theatrical act, then grew into a typical traveling railcar circus, touting the wonders of "Gentry's Equine and Canine Paradox." At its peak, the circus featured 40 ponies and 80 dogs in each of two troupes. Later, the circus grew to include other animal acts with elephants, camels, zebras, and monkeys. Dogs and ponies were still included, but it became a sideshow or a children's attraction, where kids rode the ponies and petted the dogs.

As circuses became more grand and impressive, the wagon circuses that so often featured dog and pony shows began to be viewed as "small potatoes"—small-time operations with more show than substance. Ordinary domestic animals such as dogs and ponies were no match for the impressive exotics such as alligators and tigers. Today, dogs and ponies are still part of the circus, and sometimes they are featured in acts together as part of a revival of traditional circus routines.

Feats never before
attempted by the
most intrepid aerialists!

He flies through the air with the greatest of ease, performing great tricks, bringing crowds to their knees. The acrobat is one of the most dazzling performers in the circus, his agility a marvel and his timing flawless. Regardless of his breed, your dog can perform tricks like a pro if you just stick with it, letting him build his skills slowly. Before you know it, your pup will be headed up and through the hoop, over a stick or rope, and even into your arms. Give your little star a chance to shine with these tricks that really challenge him to stretch and soar.

A great way to introduce
your dog to jumping, this trick establishes
the concept of an obstacle that must be overcome
in order to reach a treat. This is a super circus trick, and it's also a good
first step for agility training, if you want to go that route.

Setting the Stage

1 Start out with a long, straight stick and room for jumping. Measure the length between your dog's paws and his shoulders, then divide that amount by three. The final amount represents the height at which you'll need to keep the stick as you begin training. To start out, secure the stick at the determined height so it won't fall over easily.

2 Introduce the dog to the stick. Let her sniff the stick until she's comfortable, but don't let her chew it.

3 Put your dog on a leash and stand several feet in front of the stick.

Jog lightly up to the stick and jump just ahead of the dog. As you are heading toward the stick, say "Jump."

4 Lead your dog up to the stick and say, "Jump," but do not go over it yourself. If the dog goes over the stick without you, praise her.

Continue practicing the jump with your dog until she is comfortable going over.

5 Continue encouraging the dog to go over the jump, but gradually stay farther and farther away from it, allowing your dog to get accustomed to going up to and over the stick by herself.

Perfecting the Act

1 As your dog gets more comfortable going over the stick alone, you may raise the stick little by little. Never raise the stick higher than the dog can jump, and be aware that some dogs will not feel comfortable going over higher jumps.

2 Because dogs enjoy jumping so much, you probably will not need to continue treat rewards very far into the training. Be sure, however, to encourage and reward your dog with praise and affection. If she tries to go under the stick, simply lower it so that it is easier for her to go over. Once your dog has learned to jump a stick, the "Jump" command can easily be applied to other tricks as well, such as jumping through a hoop.

Best For: **Sporting, Non-Sporting, Mixed, Working**

Jump over a Stick

Jump on Trainer's Bended Back

Best For: Smaller Dogs

This trick requires a strong, flat back and a lot of work. An assistant to help manage the dog is a great help, but to be able to practice anytime and anywhere, you should be prepared to do it yourself. Be sure to use a lot of verbal praise to reward the dog's hard work.

Setting the Stage

1 You might want to use a leash to start out with to keep your dog in position for this trick. Otherwise, keep him in position by commanding "Stay," then lay down on your stomach.

2 Talk your dog into position on your back. You might do this by pointing to your back (a little awkward) and saying "Jump up" until your dog gets the picture (see figure 8). This could take time, so be patient. Praise and reward your dog when he puts any of his paws on your back and encourage him to put all four up there.

3 Once your dog understands that he should be sitting on your back, try positioning yourself on all fours and have the dog sit facing the same direction as you.

4 Tell your dog to "Jump" and guide him onto your back. This may take considerable practice.

Perfecting the Act

1 At this point, the dog needs to practice the movements of the trick. Try teaching him to jump up onto a card table (or other table that you don't mind him jumping on). You might even try getting under the table to get your dog used to the idea that he will be jumping on top of you.

2 Once he's on the table, tell him to "Sit up" so that he's not standing, but sitting on the table.

3 Once your dog is comfortable jumping onto the table, get back on all fours and have him try jumping on your back again. Be very generous with praise and treats when he accomplishes this goal.

4 From here you will begin to stand up in front of the dog. While bending over with your knees bent and your back as flat as possible, tell the dog to "Jump" and "Sit up" as you did when working with the table. Make sure that the dog sits squarely on your back.

5 With the dog on your back, gradually practice standing up straighter so that he will climb up toward your shoulders. Eventually, he'll be able to make it pretty far up your back.

Figure 8

*Performing this midair marvel is easier
for some dogs than others, but with your encouragement
and patience your dog is sure to succeed.*

Setting the Stage

1 The first thing you'll need to do is find a hoop that's the right size for your dog. He or she should be able to fit through it with ease. You can find a hoop made specifically for dogs at some pet supply stores, or use a child's hula hoop if you have a larger dog (be careful, though—a hula hoop is weighted inside, and it can become quite heavy after a lengthy training session). A good rule of thumb is to start out with a large, lightweight hoop, then move on to a smaller one later when your dog is more skilled at this trick.

2 Introduce your dog to the hoop by allowing her to look at and sniff it. If the hoop has a noisemaker inside, make sure that your dog hears it and is comfortable with it. Place the hoop flat on the ground with your dog sitting about 1 foot (30.5 cm) away, facing you and the hoop. Pat the floor or ground in the center of the hoop and

call the dog to you. When he steps inside the hoop, click, give a treat, and praise your dog.

3 After your dog has the hang of this, hold the hoop up on its edge in the jump through position, but rest it on the floor (see figure 9). Try to get the dog to walk through the hoop with a click, treat, and praise. Some timid dogs will be reluctant to step through the hoop, and may just be willing to stick their head through   for the treat. Take what you can get in the beginning and reward accordingly.

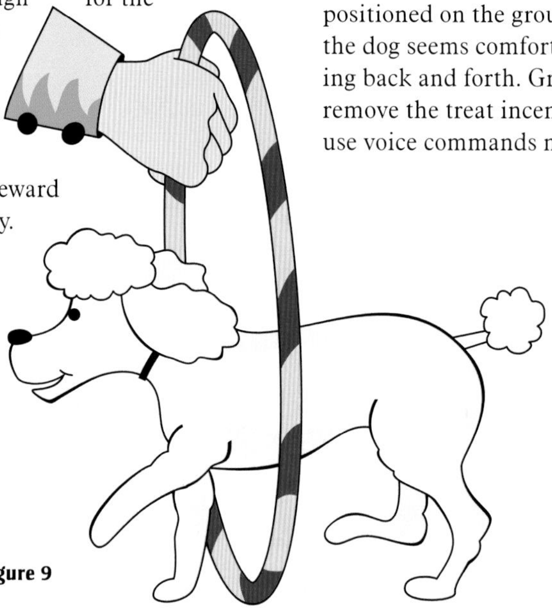

4 Hold a treat in the middle of the hoop and encourage your dog to come and get it. As the dog approaches the hoop, move your hand back a little so the dog must go all the way through. Say "Jump" as the dog moves through the hoop, and praise her appropriately. Have your dog walk through the hoop several times.

5 Continue to encourage your dog through the hoop while it's positioned on the ground until the dog seems comfortable moving back and forth. Gradually remove the treat incentive and use voice commands more often.

Figure 9

Jump through the Hoop

Perfecting the Act

1 Once your dog is comfortable going through the hoop, begin to raise it slowly. Use the "Jump" command to get the dog through the hoop. If she hesitates to jump, you may try placing the familiar stick near the bottom of the hoop as a helpful reminder of the "Jump" command.

2 When your dog successfully jumps through the hoop, vary the hoop's position and height and encourage the dog to jump through it wherever you hold it.

3 Give your dog lots of praise and encouragement for mastering this marvelous trick!

For the Superstar Dog

After you've taught your dog to go through the hoop at different heights and positions, you may try teaching the dog to jump through the hoop while someone else is holding it. Or, for a real crowd-pleaser, you can teach her to jump through the hoop with tissue paper streamers hanging down through the center of it.

Let your dog get used to the idea of the streamers on the hoop first: Show her the hoop, hold it up, and put your hand through the streamers. Some people take the trick a step further and put tissue paper over the hoop's opening, first cutting a 6- to 8-inch (15.2 to 20.3 cm) gap in the center, then gradually closing the gap until the dog happily jumps through and breaks the tissue paper. If you do decide to add this step to the trick, slit or score the paper at the place where the dog will break through (see figure 10).

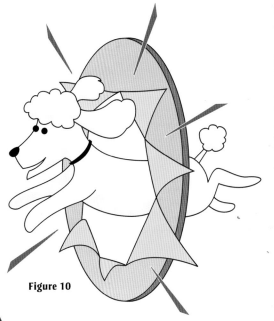

Figure 10

Talk about a showstopping trick!
As you and your dog jump rope together, you'll move in harmony,
have fun, and impress onlookers. Jumping over a rotating rope, your dog will
show off his talents not only for jumping but also for rhythm. With a little tweaking,
this can be a clown trick, as well as an acrobatic one.

Setting the Stage

1 First, practice rotating the rope without your dog. Before training begins, you'll have to learn how to keep your speed and arc consistent. It's your job to get the rope going at the right pace and to make sure that it passes under your dog while she's in the air.

2 Start by positioning your dog over the rope. As always, make sure she's comfortable with the rope before asking her to jump.

3 Rotate the rope and use the "Jump" command to get your dog to jump in the air (see figure 11). A single rotation and a jump with an ample reward is an appropriate start. It may take time to get beyond this and

Jump!

Figure 11

Best For: Sporting, Non-Sporting, Mixed, Working

Jump Rope

to get your pacing right, but don't give up. Once your dog gets used to jumping the rope, you can increase the number of jumps per session.

Perfecting the Act

Jumping is hard work. Be practical about the number of jumps you ask your dog to do at once. Even if your dog could do a hundred jumps, she'd quickly get bored. An appropriate goal to work toward is six to ten jumps at a time.

Among all dog breeds, poodles are the ones most closely associated with circus performing. With their intelligence, grace, long legs, and agility, they're naturals for a variety of tricks, from jumping to dancing to clowning. Throughout the years, poodles have been stars of the circus or novelty acts where they've often had careers spanning decades.

Dating back to early 18th-century London, records of a poodle act describe dancing for the Queen at a "Ball of Little Dogs," arranged by a dog-training impresario named Crawley. Poodles performed elaborate dramas on stage, dressed in fashionable clothing of the day, and acted out various scenes: a "lady" sitting down at a banquet table attended by dog waiters of "less aristocratic appearance," and "soldiers" attacking a toy fort.

Throughout the 19th century, poodle acts remained popular, and some gained international acclaim. Poodles distinguished themselves in every area of entertaining. Some were great acrobats—doing back somersaults in singles and doubles; others were daredevils—walking on the tightrope on their hind legs or racing a "steeplechase" with monkey riders on their backs. Some were even outfitted with boxing gloves for their forepaws and taught to spar while standing on their hind legs. A popular spectacle at the *Nouveau Cirque* in Paris featured poodles in nightdresses trapped in a flaming building awaiting rescue by poodle firemen in red coats.

But even more amazing were the dogs known for their intelligence and wit. Two famous French poodles named Philax and Brac could play dominoes "as well as any man." Professor Weiss, a famous counting and "calculating" poodle was known throughout Europe. A poodle named Bianca could "translate" and "write" in 19 languages, while another was said to be able to read, count, tell time, and describe colors. There was even a dog that was said to be able to distinguish true from false notes at the opera. Perhaps one of the best-known poodles was a "mentalist" named Munito, who dazzled crowds with his ability to mind read. In a twist on the classic card trick (see page 94), a spectator would pick a card from a deck. The dog's trainer, General Huchinson, would then spread the cards out, and Munito would pick the one the spectator had chosen. He made appearances all over Europe, touring with an "educated goat."

Even though many dog acts declined in the 20th century, poodle acts have remained popular, and poodles continue to prove themselves to be amazing entertainers, capable of just about any trick a trainer can dream up.

Skipping poodles from the Bertram Mills Circus in training for the winter season, 1959

THE DAREDEVIL

Unlock the fearless daredevil in your own dog with these time-tested tricks. Marvel as he rides the rolling barrel! Delight as he jumps into your open arms! With the proper training and a few familiar props, your dog can become a fearless entertainer, ready to wow audiences small and large with his skills and derring-do. As always, patience and consistency are the keys to successful training for these tricks. But stick with it—you (and your friends) will be amazed the first time your dog walks the plank or hops onto a skateboard for a ride—a showstopping trick for the daring-est of dogs.

Fearful frolics with fate!

Unparalleled deeds of daring!

Jump into My Arms

Who can resist giving this trick a try? It not only brings you
and your dog together, but it also builds trust between the two of you,
and of course, encourages lots of doggy kisses on your face. Before you start,
make sure that you are prepared to catch your dog and support her weight.
It helps to start training for this trick when your dog is young, because puppies
love to climb into laps and do so without much prompting.

Setting the Stage

1 Start by kneeling down and encouraging your dog to come up to your face. Extend your arms and be enthusiastic. Your dog will probably use your body like a ladder, so be prepared.

2 Ask your dog to sit and stay. Go to the other side of the room and kneel again. Call the dog with the command "Come, Up." Reward your dog with a lot of praise.

3 After your dog gets comfortable with the run and jump, begin to stand up.
Your dog will likely run and jump into your arms just for the privilege of doing so. However, if you have a hard time encouraging her to jump toward your face, try placing a treat between your lips.

Perfecting the Act

This trick requires a lot of enthusiasm and so should not be practiced more than two or three times per session. You can enhance your dog's excitement by holding a favorite toy or by calling her name.

Best For: **Sporting Group, Terrier Group, Toy Group**

Ride the Rolling Barrel

Teaching a dog to walk on top of a barrel is fairly easy with some dogs and an uphill struggle with others. Either way, the clicker will be very helpful with this trick. The bigger the diameter of the barrel, the easier it will be for the dog to balance on top. Make sure you cover the top of the barrel with a low-pile carpet to keep your dog from slipping.

Setting the Stage

If you're building your own barrel using bicycle wheels (see page 25), your finished barrel will be no more than 27 inches (69 cm) across. That's a bit of a challenge for most dogs, and you'll need to be extra patient and consistent. The training process will be much easier with a bigger barrel, and your dog will be able to take her newly learned skills and apply them to a smaller barrel later on.

1 Start by wedging small blocks of wood under the barrel keep it from rolling. If your dog is big enough to jump up onto the barrel, then get her in the sit and stay position facing the barrel. If you have a little dog, you might need to put a box or stool against the barrel to give her a boost up.

2 Once your dog is sitting and facing the barrel, pat the top of the barrel and give a suitable command, such as "Up, Up!" Some dogs will understand and jump up right away, while others will need more encouragement.

Hold a treat near the top of the barrel so your dog has to at least put her paws onto the barrel to get it. As soon as she does anything close to getting onto the barrel, click, treat, and praise. Like most tricks, the idea is to break things down into simple actions that can be combined to become the complete routine.

3 When you get to the point where the dog is standing on top of the barrel (still held in place by blocks), remove one of the blocks and use your hand or foot to keep the barrel in place. The dog should be positioned so that she could walk in place while the barrel rolls (this would be impossible if she were facing one of the open ends). If you are standing and facing the right way, then the dog will probably face you. If your dog is turning around and looking to jump down, try to get her to stay in proper position by commanding, clicking, and treating.

Best For: Terrier Group, Toy Group, Smaller Dogs

4 The barrel can roll forwards or backwards and the dog can walk forwards or backwards, so you have a lot to work with on this trick. It's usually easier to start by having the dog face you and slowly roll the barrel away from your body. Your dog will have to walk towards you as the barrel rolls away from you to keep from falling off. If you let the barrel slowly roll towards you, the dog would have to walk backwards to keep from falling off.

5 Slowly practice moving in both directions until your dog learns that she can control the speed and the direction of the barrel.

6 You will be acting as training wheels for this trick, and it will be your responsibility to keep the barrel under control by slowing it down with your hand if things get going too fast. It's important that you stay close to the action with this trick to keep the dog from falling off. A fall could be unpleasant for the dog and make her shy about getting back on, and it's possible she might get hurt. This trick takes a while to master and it's important that you don't rush things.

Perfecting the Act

1 Teaching the dog to do a pirouette on the barrel will jazz up the routine and also give the dog much more control over the barrel. If the barrel gets going too fast, an accomplished performer will do a quick turn around and use her feet to put the brakes on and get going in the other direction. Teaching the pirouette is simply a matter of leading the dog in a circle with a treat and clicking and praising as she follows the treat. A suitable command might be "Turn."

2 It's important that you face the surface of the barrel (not the open end) and that the surface on which the dog is standing is covered with low pile carpet to keep her from slipping.

Ride the Skateboard

There are two ways to get your dog to ride a skateboard:
1) you can teach the dog to stand on the skateboard and push with her paws,
or 2) you can attach a leash to the front of the skateboard and pull it along
with your dog standing on it. The pull-toy method is easier to teach (and more practical
for including in a show), but the self-propelled method is more dramatic.
Your dog will probably be the one to decide which trick is right for her.

Setting the Stage

In order to stay balanced for this trick, your dog must stand in the middle of the skateboard. You'll need to make sure the skateboard's deck is the correct scale for your dog. If the deck is too big, your dog could end up putting too much weight out to the edge, causing her to fall off. If you are working with a small dog, you'll need a small skateboard (available at most toy stores). If you have a really small dog, you may need to replace the skateboard's deck with a smaller piece of plywood. It's also important to cover the deck with low pile carpet to give your dog traction.

1 Some dogs will learn to ride a skateboard all by themselves. They will push it to get it going, then hop on for the ride. This is really funny looking and makes a great crowd-pleasing trick, but

has some practical limitations. You'll need a big enough space for the dog to get going, but not so big that the dog will end up too far from center stage. There are also safety concerns—you don't want the dog to be able to roll into a dangerous place, such as onto the stairs or into traffic. If you do want to try to train your dog to do the self-propelled method, the clicker will be useful. You'll need to click to let the dog know that you want her to push with one or two paws

and keep the others on the deck of the skateboard (see figure 12). When she does this, click to distinctly mark the desired behavior, then praise, and treat. If your dog masters the pushing part, you can add the next two steps: standing on the board with all fours, and going for a little ride. With time, your dog will realize that in order to go for the ride, she first has to push and then jump on. It's a lot to ask of the dog, but it's been done.

Best For: Any

Figure 12

2 For the pull method, you just need to train the dog to stay on the skateboard and shift her balance as the skateboard moves and turns. Your job is to make it as easy as possible for the dog to stay on—that means slow, smooth starts and stops and wide, gentle turns.

Give your dog lots of praise and the occasional treat for staying on the skateboard. Using the clicker can create confusion with this trick as there is no real "pinpoint" moment for you to click to mark the desired behavior. Most dogs will catch on that you want them to stay on the skateboard and will as long as they are having fun and are in a cooperative mood.

Walking along a narrow board is an easy trick for a dog to learn, but it won't be very impressive to an audience unless there is a danger factor. You could create a sense of danger by placing the plank higher off the ground, but you certainly would not want to do put your dog in real danger. Instead, try presenting this as a comedy bit, with a comedic and silly sense of danger. Place a few toy cats or squeaky toys under the plank and make a big fuss about the risk of falling into a pit of bloodthirsty kittens or some such silliness.

Setting the Stage

1 Start with a wide board to make the training easy for the dog. Later, work down to a narrower board to make the trick more dramatic and "dangerous" looking.

Depending on the size of your dog, you'll need a board between 4 to 12 inches (10.2 x 30.5 cm) wide and 4 to 8 feet (122 x 244 cm) long. You can suspend the board off the ground by placing it on overturned buckets (heavy-duty 5-gallon [19 l] buckets can be found at home improvement stores). You might need to secure the board to the buckets so the dog doesn't push the board off as she is trying to get on. This can be done by drilling through the ends of the board and through the bucket, then securing the pieces together with a carriage bolt and wing

nut. Paint the buckets to look like circus props, if you like, and cover the board with low pile carpet to make it non-slip for your dog.

2 You'll need to break the trick down into segments. First, teach the dog to hop up onto the board. Pat the surface where you want her to go and give a command like "Up, Up" or the all purpose international circus term "Hup!" If your dog does anything that moves her towards getting on the board (such as putting even one paw on it), click, praise, and treat. Once your dog is standing on the board, hold a treat out in front of her nose so she'll walk along and follow the treat.

Best For: Any

Walk the Plank

Figure 13

If she does it, click, praise, and give her the treat (see figure 13). If she jumps off the board, give her a firm, but gentle "No, no." When your dog is on the board and walking along nicely, you can stand close enough so that if she starts to jump off, you can use your hand to stop her and guide her back along the board.

When your dog gets to the end of the plank, train her to stay there and wait for a command to jump off. This is a good time for a "Ta Daa!" moment where you will cue the audience that it is time to applaud. If there is applause, you can then give the command for the dog to jump off the plank and then make an even bigger "Ta Daa!"

Climb the Ladder and Jump to Me

Here's a feat of doggy daring if ever there was one.
Climbing a ladder can be very tricky for little paws, and the space
between the rungs can seem huge to a dog. Take your time with this trick,
and don't expect instant progress. When your dog does get it down,
though, you and your audience will be amazed.

You may want to start out with a short stepladder with wide steps for this trick. A bad experience (such as a fall) early on will discourage your dog and may prevent her from trying again.

Setting the Stage

1 Start by approaching the ladder (you may want to have your dog on the leash for this part). Pat the first step, and command "Climb." Your dog will probably put her paw onto the first rung (see figure 14). Getting her to put her paw onto the next rung

Figure 14

may be a bit more difficult. Command "Climb," and lift one paw onto the second rung.

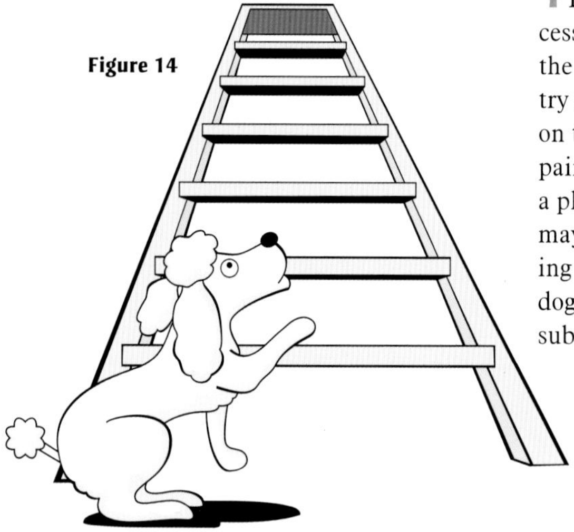

2 When your dog has made it up a few steps, click, praise, and reward. Make sure you are very effusive in your praise every time your dog takes another step upward.

3 Don't push your dog too hard on the first try with this trick. It may take quite a few training sessions to get your dog all the way to the top.

4 If you are successful with the stepladder, try moving on to a steady painter's ladder with a platform on top. You may need to start training over again if your dog is confused by the substitute ladder.

Best For: Sporting Group, Working Group

Perfecting the Act

Once she's climbing to the top, you may want to teach your dog to jump off the platform of the ladder (make sure she learns to do it on your command, rather than climbing up to the top and jumping off on her own—a recipe for disaster).

In the sensational world of the circus, it could be hard for a humble canine to compete with the more exotic animal stars of the show—lions, elephants, and camels, for example. To make an impact, dogs were often called upon to perform extraordinary deeds of daring. Animal trainers took advantage of the natural inclination of some dogs and breeds to jump and climb to create breathtaking circus acts.

Performing "feats scarcely less than human," dogs were trained to walk on tight wires, dive from platforms, and of course, jump through flaming hoops. Rexie, "the sensational high diver," could climb a 40-foot (12 m) ladder, then jump from a platform into a blanket held below. "Shady the Mexican Wonder Dog" (a Mexican hairless) could climb a 30-foot-tall (9 m) ladder and walk across a 25-

Left: Rexie, the Sensational High Diver, caught mid-jump.

Right: Rambling Gold, the champion dog jumper makes the world-record high jump of the canine world, reaching a height of 12 feet, 2 inches. The English coursing hound was owned by John Drake. Circa 1916.

"REXIE"
The Sensational High Diver 40 feet

2581

foot-long (8 m) wire, then jump into the arms of his trainer below. How were such marvels possible? The trainers followed the same techniques you would use to train your own dog, but gradually ratcheted up the heights and distances. Just like human athletes, the dogs built up specific muscles for performing specific tricks, and improved their precision with repetition.

While these sorts of acts started to die out with the consolidation of the circus field from many small "mom and pop" circuses into a handful of larger ones, daredevil dog acts continue to be an attraction in and of themselves, with dogs performing "extreme" tricks and stunts at festivals, half-time shows, and theme parks.

A long-forgotten act: doggie head straddling

Shady, the Mexican Wonder Dog and Hairless Gymnast, was the star of the Hayes Werntz Circus.

Fabulous frolics!

THE
CLOWN

Immensely funny business!

All the world loves a clown dog, a charming entertainer who keeps everyone in stitches with his amusing antics. Clown dogs have been a standard act in the circus (and rodeo) for ages, showing up their human counterparts with their clever tricks and impeccable comic timing. They love to get a laugh and feed on applause from a crowd. Your dog can take part in this great tradition by becoming skilled at just a few funny moves that you'll learn in this chapter. Try them out and get a feel for your dog's comic style—is she the slapstick type, or does he like to play straight man to your buffoon? Once you've got a few tricks down, you can invent your own, playing to your dog's own strengths. Get ready for lots of fun and lots of laughs.

Do the Crawl

Best For: Hound Group, Terrier Group, Sporting or Non-Sporting Group

The crawl doesn't require much comic genius on the part of your dog—it's just naturally funny to look at. Once your dog realizes this trick will get him praise and applause, he'll be eager to perform it again and again.

Setting the Stage

The dog must be proficient in the "Down" command to make this work. For this trick, you need a low table or a bench that the dog can crawl under.

1 Give your dog the "Down" command so that her head is near the front of the table. Reach under the table with a treat in hand and guide her to follow along. With any luck, she'll start to stretch to reach the treat. As soon as that happens, say "Crawl," and reward her with praise (see figure 15).

2 Gradually guide your dog further under the table with the treat. If the table is low enough, it will prevent the dog from standing up. When the dog comes out from under the table

(even if she doesn't make it all the way to the end), praise and reward her (see figure 16). Continue this process until she's comfortable crawling under the table.

3 Next, have your dog lie down on one side of the table and ask her to stay. Go to the other side and kneel down so you can see your dog.

4 Introduce the "Come, Crawl" command to encourage the dog to crawl toward you.
Once the dog makes it all the way to the other side of the table, be prepared for her to stand up. Encourage your dog to stay down longer and longer by withholding praise until she crawls a little farther.

Figure 16

Perfecting the Act

1 As your dog learns to crawl, you can stop using the "Come" command and just use "Crawl." You can also remove the table and encourage the dog to crawl without it.

2 If your dog has trouble staying down without the table, or does not want to go under it at all, you can use your hand to apply very slight pressure to the shoulder blades as a reminder that the crawl must be performed in a down position. Be sure to work yourself gradually into a standing position so that the dog will learn the command even if you're not kneeling next to her.

Figure 15

This is one of those tricks that's funny because it puts the dog in the position of doing something humans usually do: unrolling a carpet runner. It's even funnier because he's doing it with his nose.

Setting the Stage

1 Have your dog sit and stay while facing you, and show him that you are placing a yummy treat about 1 foot (30.5 cm) from the edge of the rug. Fold the 1-foot (30.5 cm) portion of the rug over the treat. This is a great exercise in maintaining the "Sit" and "Stay" commands because the dog is likely to want to go right after the concealed treat, but he'll need to wait until you give the "Get it" command. At that point, most dogs will use their snoot to flip the rug over to expose the treat.

2 Try this a few times, and then fold the end of the rug over twice, burying the treat under two layers of carpet. Pretty soon, your dog will be unrolling as much of the carpet as necessary to get at the treat. Unless you are trying to use a room-size piece of wall-to-wall carpet, this is an easy task for a dog.

3 Once your dog starts to push the rolled-up rug, a certain amount of momentum will take over, and the dog won't have to push very hard.

Perfecting the Act

Once the dog is dependably unrolling the rug, you can start to leave out the "buried" treat and then hand the dog a treat after the rug is unrolled. This trick is so easy that you probably won't even need to use the clicker because the dog will figure out for himself how to get a treat.

Best For: **Hound Group, Sporting Group**

Unroll the Carpet Runner

Do the Weave

This is an impressive trick, combining the agility skills of an acrobat and the comic timing of a clown. You'll teach your dog to weave in and out of your legs as you walk slowly. Because your dog must bend around the neck and shoulders quite a bit, it's not the ideal trick for a rapidly growing puppy or an older dog with arthritis. You, too, will be bending and twisting a lot, so if your back's not too strong, you might try teaching your dog to weave through poles or hoops instead of your legs.

Setting the Stage

1 Start by having your dog heel at your side. Take a big step forward with your right leg only.

2 Hold a treat between your legs and command "Through, weave." Reward your dog with the treat and repeat until she's comfortable going through your legs (see figure 17).

3 Next, use a treat to lead her once around your left leg and back through again, completing a circle.

4 Once your dog will go all the way around your left leg, use a treat to lead the dog around your right leg and back through again. This will complete the weave pattern.

Figure 17

Best For: **Sporting Group, Non-Sporting Group, Herding Group**

Perfecting the Act

1 Continue practicing the "Through, Weave" command while slowly switching the command to just "Weave." Also, encourage your dog to weave without a treat reward. Make sure your dog is very comfortable with weaving before moving on.

2 Each time your dog circles a leg, move the opposite leg forward. Begin this very slowly by guiding your dog with your hands.

3 If your dog doesn't get confused, gradually begin to pick up the pace until her motion becomes more fluid. If your dog does get confused, take it more slowly. This takes a lot of practice, so be patient.

4 Be careful not to go too fast because your dog must be able to get all the way around your leg for each step. Also, make sure your dog keeps her head down. You don't want the dog to move you, lift you, or bowl you over with your legs spread so far apart. You'll need to practice a lot to bring all the elements together.

The Shell Game

In this classic trick, your dog will display his "mentalist" powers by finding a hidden treat in an upside-down bowl. The dog's powerful scenting abilities make this a foolproof trick, but the audience is meant to think your keen-eyed dog followed the action of your hands. You'll need three unbreakable bowls—plastic flowerpots work particularly well, but you can even use plastic cups. Use particularly strong-smelling treats for this trick, such as hotdog bits or freeze-dried liver.

Setting the Stage

1 Sit on a smooth floor surface with one bowl, pot, or cup. Have your dog sit in front of you.

2 Place a treat under an inverted container and tell your dog to "Find it." Tip the container a little so your dog can nose the crack between the bowl and the floor (see figure 18).

3 Praise your dog and let her have the treat.

4 After several training sessions, begin putting the container flat on the floor and encouraging your dog to paw or nose it. Don't give her the treat until she makes a very visible sign indicating where the treat is.

Perfecting the Act

1 Invert a second container with nothing under it and place it next to the one you've been working with. Put a treat under the working container.

2 Encourage your dog to find the treat, using the "Find it" command. When your dog indicates the correct bowl, reward her with the treat and praise.

3 At this point, you'll want to start mixing up the container placement to encourage your dog to use her nose to sniff out the treat. Make sure she watches you put the treat under the bowl so that it creates the illusion of a keen-eyed dog.

Figure 18

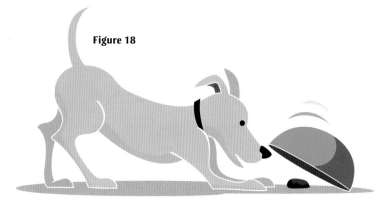

Best For: Hound Group, Sporting Group

4 After she gets comfortable with two bowls, add a third and begin to mix them up more thoroughly—she'll have no problem locating the treat.

5 After your dog knows the trick, you can put different objects under the bowl. Favorite chew toys work well. Be sure to keep the training upbeat, and don't train too much at a time. It's important to stop while the dog is excited because that excitement will transfer over to the following training sessions. Remember, always leave the dog wanting more.

Bring a Basket

Best For: Sporting Group, Non-Sporting Group, Terrier Group, Hound Group

While not strictly a clown-type trick, this one has great comic possibilities—dogs just look funny carrying unexpected things. It's easy to teach a dog to bring a basket to you as long as you are working with a "brings things" kind of dog. Dogs who love to play fetch or tug with doggy toys will quickly learn to bring things to you on command. If you are working with a non-fetcher, this trick is less successful.

Setting the Stage

1 If your dog is truly a fetcher, teaching him to bring a basket may be as simple as holding the basket up to his mouth. When he takes it, click and praise. If you try to give him a treat, your dog will drop the basket to take the treat. If your dog has a favorite toy that he likes to bring to you for a game of fetch or tug, you can start to use a command such as "Bring it" as the dog is getting the toy. This command will be easy to transfer to the basket or non-toy object that you want the dog to bring.

2 Dogs who aren't interested in toys and don't carry things around on their own will have difficulty with this trick. You'll have to try to build the behavior a step at a time by first teaching the dog to hold an object in his mouth until given the command to release it (see figure 19). When the dog can achieve that first step, you'll combine holding the object with the "Sit," "Stay," and "Come" commands. If successful, your dog will bring the basket to you on cue. Very often, though, dogs that show no interest in fetching or tugging will not take to this trick, and some will just plain not want to do it.

Figure 19

Perfecting the Act

If you're performing the trick for a crowd, you may want to put something inside the basket for additional comic value—some food item that the dog will then proceed to remove from the basket and eat (it's funnier if it's your lunch), something embarrassing (a toupee, for example), or an inherently funny item.

The Amazing
Card Shark

Your dog will shock and amaze a crowd with his ability to "read" cards. This magic trick requires a bit of sleight of hand on your part, as well as some special equipment. Once you've got it down, though, it's sure to be an audience favorite.

Setting the Stage

1 The easiest way to pull this off is to teach your dog to pick a single playing card out of a bag that has been set up with two compartments. You can either make the bag yourself or buy a trick bag at a magic shop.

2 The trick goes like this. You hold up a pack of cards and ask a member of your audience to select one card. When the card has been chosen, you slip the deck back into the bag, letting the chosen card fall to one side and the rest of the deck to the other. This will take some skill (and practice) on your part. Once the selected card has been separated from the rest of the

deck, seal off the compartment holding the whole deck so that the one with the single card is the only one that's accessible (any book on performing magic tricks will have diagrams on how to set this up). Your dog will then put his snoot down into the compartment containing the single selected card and pick it out. It will appear to the audience as if your dog has pulled the chosen card out of a big pile of cards (see figure 20).

Figure 20

Best For: **Hound Group, Sporting Group, Non-Sporting Group**

Perfecting the Act

This trick will have much more of an impact if you make a big spiel to the audience about your dog and his amazing mental powers. You may even want to put him in a little cape for more dramatic effect.

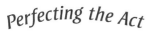

Dog Stars

Pete the Pup—Superstar Dog

Perhaps one of the most famous performing dogs ever, Pete the Pup, a Staffordshire terrier, is still remembered today for his distinctive look and his role in the classic television series, *Little Rascals*. Pete the Pup, otherwise known as "The Dog with the Ring Around His Eye," won the hearts of a generation—every kid in the United States in the 1930s wanted a dog like Pete. He was born with a natural ring around his eye, but it was enhanced for the screen by famous Hollywood makeup artist Max Factor. Pete's trainer, Harry Lucenay, taught him to pull a wagon, stand on his hind legs while balancing a ball on his nose, and many other tricks. Pete's life came to an untimely end when he was poisoned by an unknown assailant. But his memory lives on in celluloid, and he even has his own star on the Hollywood Walk of Fame.

The beloved mascot of the *Little Rascals*, Pete was not only a great actor, he could perform stunts, too.

A veritable
vision!

Marvelous
acts of grace,
ease, and
perfection!

While "dancing" has long been the domain of the poodle, there are lots of other breeds with the energy, intelligence, and leg strength to tackle this specialized skill. Once your dog has mastered the art of standing on his hind legs, the sky's the limit—he can be taught to spin, move forward, or even dance with other dogs. It may take your dog some time to make progress on this trick, but don't give up too easily. If you stick with it, you'll be rewarded with a truly astounding performance that will amaze and dazzle your friends!

DANCERS

Dance on Hind Legs

For a dog, the first step in learning to dance is to stand on hind legs and move about. This trick requires an athletic dog and a great deal of practice building up hind leg muscles. Don't start this trick with a young pup—the action may cause stress to his growing bones. It's equally unsuitable for older or arthritic dogs. It's great, though, for strong healthy dogs who enjoy a good work out.

Setting the Stage

1 Start with your dog in the "Sit up" or "Beg" position.

2 Hold a treat above your dog's head, just out of reach. Reward your dog for any attempt to reach the treat. Make sure that you give the treat while his front legs are still in the air, however, so he starts to understand the trick (see figure 21).

3 If your dog attempts to jump for the treat, ignore that behavior and don't reward him. Instead, ask him to sit and start over.

4 As your dog starts standing higher and higher for the treat, add the command "Dance."

5 When he finally gets up all the way on his hind legs, begin to extend the length of time during which he balances.

Remember, your dog's muscles need conditioning. Three seconds is a long time for a dog to balance in the upright position when he's just beginning, so don't expect too much too soon.

Figure 21

Perfecting the Act

1 Once your dog starts to get the hang of the trick and develops his leg and hip muscles, try moving the treat around before rewarding the dog. This will encourage the dog to take steps, which start to look a little like dancing.

2 This trick is particularly difficult, so be sure to use really good treats that your dog gets excited about. Also, body posture is integral to this trick. The dog's head must be over the thorax, the thorax over the hips, and the hips over the hindquarters. There must be a straight line down the dog's back to maintain the proper balance, and the front legs must be tucked close to the body.

Best For: Sporting Group, Terrier Group, Working Group

You can give a "Twirl" command, or even teach the dog to turn left and right, by simply extending the trick on page 100.

Setting the Stage

1 After your dog has learned to balance on his hind legs and can move a little bit, use a circular hand gesture and the command "Twirl" to encourage the dog to move in a circular motion (see figure 22).

2 Or teach the dog to walk with you by holding a treat in front of the dog, or by guiding him as you walk along beside him. As you walk, say "Right turn," and make a sharp right turn. The dog will start to follow you and will learn the command (see figure 23). Then practice "Left turn" in the same fashion.

Perfecting the Act

Fade out the food reward as soon as possible because it becomes difficult to administer while walking. Instead, use your hand as a target and give the dog verbal praise.

Figure 22

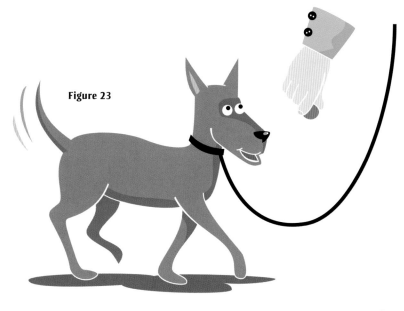

Figure 23

Best For: Sporting Group, Terrier Group, Working Group

Dance around

Pirouette on Hind Legs

Some dogs are natural hind-leg stander-uppers, and some
are built strictly for all-fours. The low-to-the-ground basset hound
type isn't going to win any dance contests, and a dachshund might actually
suffer a back injury from hind-leg standing. Most of the natural hind-leg standers will
do it on their own if it gets them closer to a treat. You'll need patience (and your dog
will need strong hind legs) to master this trick, which builds on the skills learned
training for the Dance on Hind Legs or Dance around tricks (see pages 100 and 102).

Setting the Stage

1 Give the "Dance" command (see page 101) to get your dog onto his hindquarters.

2 If he holds that position for a moment, he will naturally start to do a quarter turn. Encourage that spin, and lead it with a treat.

3 Lead the spin in very small circles and increase the spin as you say "Pirouette," or, as with the other trick, "Twirl" (see figure 24).

Figure 24

Perfecting the Act

Gradually increase the period of time that the dog pirouettes to about three or four rotations.

For the Superstar Dog

Once your dog has the hang of the trick, consider adding music or costumes. Feel free to dress up your dog in a costume and play music to make this trick part of a real audience-capturing show.

Best For: Sporting Group, Terrier Group, Working Group

Dog Stars

Dancing with Your Star

Let's say your dog really takes to these dancing tricks. You're amazed by her agility, her sense of rhythm, and her timing. You can't resist dancing with her, and before you know it, the two of you are like Fred and Ginger, cutting a rug, making up new steps, and even coming up with a routine. You may think that you're the only human-canine team to explore the world of dance, but you're actually part of a movement that's sweeping the continent: Canine Musical Freestyle.

According to Patie Ventre, the founder of the World Canine Freestyle Association, musical freestyle is "a choreographed musical program performed by handlers and their dogs,

displaying the dog and handler in a creative, innovative, and original dance, using music and intricate movements to show-case teamwork, artistry, cos-tuming, athleticism, and style in interpreting the theme of the music." In other words, it's dancing with your dog for fun, entertainment, bonding, and health benefits.

This new sport developed in the United States and Canada during the early 1990s. It combines elements of obedi-ence training and dressage. Instead of moving through the typical components of a training routine, though, dog and owner perform a three- to six-minute act in time to music, complete with costumes and props. En-thusiasts say it's more fun to do than typical obedience training, and spectators agree that it's definitely more fun to watch.

The first canine freestyle competition took place in 1993, and the sport has been growing ever since. There are now clubs all over the United States and Canada, many of which offer demonstrations and workshops to introduce newcomers to the joy of dancing with your dog.

You can find out more about canine musical freestyle by visiting www.worldcaninefree-style.org.

The Trick Dogs Show

Rick Martin

Chico

Twinky

Comet

About the Performers

Rick Martin has been a professional variety artist for many years and has entertained throughout the United States and Canada. Before adopting his troop of performing dogs, Rick earned a living as a comedy magician and ventriloquist.

Chico was adopted by Rick in early 1999 from an animal shelter in Broward County, Florida. He was a homeless stray, captured in the wilds of Fort Lauderdale by animal control agents. Most people think he looks like he might be part Corgi, but Chico claims to be a mutant form of giant Chihuahua.

Comet, a Rat Terrier, joined the family a few months after Chico. Rick found him in the back room of the Monroe County, Florida animal shelter, in a cage labeled "fear biter." Comet was not considered a candidate for adoption. And, after being adopted by Rick, it was several weeks before he would let him touch him at all. Comet regained his trust in people and confidence in himself, and he is living proof of the healing power of love.

Twinky joined the show in the Spring of 1999 and she also is a graduate of the Monroe County shelter. Twinky appears to be a Rat Terrier, and like Comet, was a family pet that didn't work out. Twinky is very modest, but the rest of the family recognizes her as the "brains of the outfit." Lucy, a wild and crazy Jack Russell Terrier, joined the act in the spring of 2002. Lucy

had been adopted and returned several times by families who were unable to keep up with her appetite for activity. Performing with The Tricky Dogs Show is a great outlet for Lucy's excess energy.

Peewee T. Poodle joined the act in the Fall of 2005. He's very smart and extra cute and a great playmate for Lucy. Peewee was given to Rick because his previous owners thought Peewee the poodle would enjoy being in show biz, and he certainly does. Peewee closes the act with his Amazing Doggy Daredevil Dive of Doom.

Lucy

Peewee T. Poodle

Acknowledgments

The editorial team would like to thank the lovely and talented Susan Kieffer and the magnificent David Squires for all their help with research and writing. Much applause goes to the astonishing art director, Kristi Pfeffer, who performed heretofore unimagined feats of creativity; illustrious illustrator, Orrin Lundgren; sensational set designer Ben Betsalel; and photo stylists extraordinaire Chris Bryant and Skip Wade; and, last but not least, photographer Steve Mann. And of course, a big "bravo" to the stars of our show, Rick Martin and The Tricky Dogs, who thrill and delight with their sparkling showmanship.

Photo Credits

Page 10 (clockwise, from top left):
© Brand X Pictures, ©istockphoto.com/Ira Bachinskya, ©istockphoto.com/Erik Lam, ©istockphoto.com/Fanelle Rosier

Page 11 (clockwise, from top left):
©istockphoto.com/John Long, ©istockphoto.com/Kit Sen Chin, ©istockphoto.com/Chris Hellyar, ©istockphoto.com/Tad Denson

Page 12 (clockwise, from top left):
©istockphoto.com/Jason Lugo, ©istockphoto.com/Lauren Rinder, ©istockphoto.com/Mike Jones, ©istockphoto.com/Justin Horrocks, ©istockphoto.com/Erik Lam

Page 23 (clockwise, from top left):
© Royalty-free/comstock.com, © Royalty-Free/Corbis, © Royalty-Free/Corbis

Page 30 (left to right):
©istockphoto.com/Ira Bachinskya, © Royalty-Free/comstock.com

Page 31 (left to right):
©istockphoto.com/Jennifer Matthews, ©istockphoto.com/Leah-Anne Thompson

Page 34:
© Royalty-Free/Corbis

Page 46:
©The Gary Bart Photo Archive

Page 47:
© Vintage Images/Getty Images

Page 48-49:
© GK Hart/Vikki Hart/Getty Images

Page 61:
© Hulton Archive/Getty Images; Photo by Ron Chase

Page 62-63:
©Nick North/Corbis

Page 78 (left to right):
©The Gary Bart Photo Archive, © Hulton Archive/Getty Images

Page 79:
both images ©The Gary Bart Photo Archive

Page 80:
© Royalty-Free/Corbis

Page 81:
© Royalty-Free/Corbis

Page 97:
© Hulton Archive/Getty Images

Page 98-99:
© Brand X Pictures

Metric Equivalents

Inches	Centimeters	Inches	Centimeters
1/8	3 mm	12	30
1/4	6 mm	13	32.5
3/8	9 mm	14	35
1/2	1.3	15	37.5
5/8	1.6	16	40
3/4	1.9	17	42.5
7/8	2.2	18	45
1	2.5	19	47.5
1 1/4	3.1	20	50
1 1/2	3.8	21	52.5
1 3/4	4.4	22	55
2	5	23	57.5
2 1/2	6.25	24	60
3	7.5	25	62.5
3 1/2	8.8	26	65
4	10	27	67.5
4 1/2	11.3	28	70
5	12.5	29	72.5
5 1/2	13.8	30	75
6	15	31	77.5
7	17.5	32	80
8	20	33	82.5
9	22.5	34	85
10	25	35	87.5
11	27.5	36	90

Index